THE MANAGER'S GUIDE TO
BECOMING
GREAT

LAWRENCE PINGREE

iUniverse, Inc.
Bloomington

The Manager's Guide to Becoming Great

iUniverse books may be ordered through booksellers or by contacting:

iUniverse
1663 Liberty Drive
Bloomington, IN 47403
www.iuniverse.com
1-800-Authors (1-800-288-4677)

ISBN: 978-0-595-47786-9 (sc)
ISBN: 978-0-595-61691-6 (hc)
ISBN: 978-1-4620-4910-3 (e)

Printed in the United States of America

iUniverse rev. date: 8/12/2011

Contents

Foreword

This book is dedicated to my parents. My mother, Cheryl Ann Pingree, passed before I had a chance to tell her how important she was to my life and how much I loved her. Cheryl was a wonderful, caring mother who only did the best for me in my life and for our family. We miss her and love her always. She was an inspiration to many other people and highly regarded as a good natured, honest, thoughtful and funny person.

My father, to whom I am grateful for the love and support he has provided over the years, has always been there for me in tough times and he's picked me up and assured me that things will be okay. My Grandfather, Owen F. Cooper, taught me how to drive, took care of me after school, let me play with his CB radio, and took me out for walks in the mountains. I will never forget those days. I love you completely.

Thanks to everyone else who provided me guidance throughout my life; I appreciate everything everyone has done for me.

Special Acknowledgements

I would like to recognize the following people, who made this book possible or provided the necessary guidance:

- Bob Bailey (Gilroy, CA)—you were there for me when I needed a second opinion and have always been a great friend.

- Suzanne Widup (Livermore, CA)—for being there for me while I went through the toughest times in my life. You're a great friend and colleague.

- Dan Schooler (San Diego, CA)—without the things that you and I had gone through together in Silicon Valley and as young adults, this book would not have been possible. Thanks Dan!

- Steven Britton (San Diego, CA)—If it wasn't for the opportunity you and your brother brought to my life, I would not stand where I am today without your friendship. Thanks Steve!

- Woody Hughes (Discovery Bay, CA)—through our discussions, you provided a wonderful wealth of information about managers that helped me see some of the topics that I should discuss. Thank you!

Introduction

The purpose of this book is to illustrate the common problems and possible solutions associated with managing people. It is designed to be the first book a new manager picks up, so that he or she can properly learn the basics of management, create a successful team, and be viewed as a qualified leader.

After reading this book, you will have a solid understanding of the important concepts of management. It should enable you with a "common sense" view of management, a view that every great leader needs to be successful. If you want to be perceived as "great" then you need to do certain things to make that happen and this book is designed to show you how.

For the experienced manager, take this book and place it in your desk drawer.

When having a difficult moment, grab it to review the concepts contained within to help guide your decisions by reviewing possibilities you may not have considered. In the course of my life I've found research to be an invaluable tool when frustrated by circumstances. My life and my experiences have changed in very positive ways through its use. Information is the power by which humans run.

1

Management Responsibilities

CHAPTER OBJECTIVES:

- Determine what it means to be a manager

- Learn how to avoid some of the common mistakes in management

- Analyze the duties and responsibilities common to all management positions

The first promotion

From the first day on the job as a manager you are confronted with many problems and situations requiring your immediate attention and quick response. Your problems multiply at a rapid rate, and you may begin to desire to be back in the old position where your duties were actually pretty easy. Now a wrong decision, a careless remark, a violation of human relations can take months to correct. You suddenly become aware of the fact that you are up against some major issues. The job of managing others is not as easy as it seemed when you were only responsible for your own production.

Many people can't take this new responsibility and the hardships that come along with it. They find their new management duties too worrying, confusing, demanding, uncomfortable, and downright unpleasant. These people often end up requesting to be returned to their old position where they were only responsible for their own output. They enjoyed it more when someone else told them exactly what to do and when it had to be completed.

Other people are too weak, timid, unintelligent, immature, or they may lack other attributes of leadership required in a management position. Generally, they too end up losing their chance when a promotion becomes available. It is fairly obvious who can handle the task of management as it takes a certain type of personality, one with maturity and a drive to excellence and execution.

Being an expert craftsman, engineer, analyst, or typist does not guarantee that one will become a great manager. Sometimes a person who is a very poor or lazy employee in lower positions turns out to be a very great manager. Why you ask?

Because they understand how to get more work out of others, and how to get along well with people while maintaining discipline. Many people lack the understanding that getting along with people is the most important attribute to attain and it is this attribute alone that limits them.

The ability to get others to work for you willingly is so important that a good deal of time in any management training course should be devoted to the subject of "Human Relations," which is the art of getting along with other people. If you lack the soft skills that are necessary to lead a team, the results of that are going to be disastrous for you and your future as a manager.

Defining the roles: Manager and Employee

A manager's primary deliverables in the workplace is to manage the team's bud-get, time allocations, work unit allocations, inter-departmental issues, and to ensure task execution. So now that you are responsible for the output of others, you seldom perform the actual production work yourself except when absolutely necessary.

You must devise creative ways to get a good day's work out of others. Keep in mind that everything you do or say can affect everything you and your group do as well as everyone's combined productivity. This is the daily worry of every manager. Psychology is an important aspect to consider on a daily basis.

There is a fine line between being a manager and being an employee. Remember, the employee does not see you as an equal, so be cognizant of this fact and consider it in each interaction with your employees.

On the other hand, employees are responsible for execution. Their job is to take tasks given by a manager, and ensure the execution of the overall goal given by executive staff. It is the employees who complete the most important tasks, so treat them respectfully and with admiration as they are your bread and butter and your life blood as a manager. You are the leader; they will follow if you become one.

Getting people to work hard

Getting work out of others is not as simple today as it was in the past. In the past, the manager was the fellow who could dominate every man in their team due to being brawnier or more aggressive. These old "crack-the-whip" tactics have no place in today's leadership. The manager who tries to push employees by threats of termination or other disciplinary actions does not get very far.

Your employees know pretty well that you can terminate them. In fact it's in the back of almost every employee's mind every time you interact with them, and they are reminding themselves of it each time you even marginally criticize them.

Using this tactic is more likely to create a rebellion and lower the productivity of your team than to actually cause more work to be performed.

The old aggressive type of management is no longer acceptable. Today's need is for leaders who have the ability to inspire their people to work because they want to work. People will produce to the extent that they like and respect their management.

Your instructions or direction should not be executed without careful consideration of their feelings. Your direction should keep in mind that most employees want to please you. If you congratulate your employees when they accomplish tasks, you'll have a very grateful and productive staff.

Common initial mistakes

Those first days on your new "management" job are mighty important ones to you. Your fellow employees will be watching you to see how you react to this new responsibility. If you are promoted within your own group, it is particularly difficult to avoid antagonizing your former associates who often are jealous of your promotion.

Your management also will be watching you closely. It is likely, too, that the other managers around you will be observing and reporting your actions to your management.

When you move into this role or any job, the best bet for you is to be as quiet and inconspicuous as possible, at least until you get your feet on the ground.

Maintain a calm, friendly, quiet attitude. Listen carefully to others. Make it a rule to keep your ears open and your mouth shut during this period of transition, it will pay off greatly later.

Now let's take a look at some of the common mistakes made by new managers. Any one of them can cause you months of trouble, breakdown of morale in your unit, unpopularity, or a complete loss of your rate. Avoid these mistakes.

"New Broom" tactics are out! It is quite common to see inexperienced managers go into their new job with the idea that "things must change here." They want to make a "big show". They let it be known that they did not like the way the last manager operated. They often want to wipe the slate clean and start all over!

They have forgotten a very potent psychological factor called "Resistance to Change". People resent and fear change. Experienced managers going into a new organization start out by letting everyone know that nothing will be changed for the time being. They tell their staff that everything presently in effect will remain in effect and that no changes in personnel, equipment, procedures, etc., are planned.

Once you get your feet on the ground, you can gradually make necessary changes. During this phase, ensure that you carefully socialize the changes to your group and that there is a clear understanding why you are making the change; you will cause dissent if you don't prepare them psychologically.

Making promises during this period is also particularly foolish. In an effort to win friends, new managers often make rash promises that are unrealistic. The promise to help someone win a promotion or obtain a pay raise, even if only implied or hinted at, is like dynamite to others. Many managers who foolishly promised something at one time or another will tell you they lived to wish that they could have "eaten their words".

Sometimes the powers you think you now have are not so easily exercised without the cooperation of the HR department, so keep in mind that the final word may not be yours. Employees will not care when you try to explain that your efforts were vetoed; they will only know—and remember—that you made a promise and failed to follow through.

Dictatorial practices, particularly with former co-workers you had disliked, are resented fiercely. Any show of authority will be particularly noticed during the first days on a job. Our nation is a democracy and most Americans are imbued with antagonism toward tyranny both at home and abroad.

Playing favorites, being partial to former friends, ignoring employees who are timid or backward, and assigning the best jobs to the chosen few will rapidly break down the morale of the whole department. Managers who play favorites often find themselves losing the support of even their former friends.

Careless remarks, which would go unnoticed if they came from a non-man-ager, take on new significance when they come from a manager. The new manager, who now represents management to their employees, is going to have to start weighing each word that is spoken. Employees are quick to pick up careless remarks made by a manager and interpret them as official policy or worse. These days, a careless remark can also put you in court.

Trying to do all the work yourself, failing to delegate work, and fearing to trust your team are common failings of a new or unseasoned manager. You can always tell this type because they soon become so "stacked up" with work that they bottleneck the whole department. Experienced managers have learned that with a little trusting and proper training, their employees can usually do the job as well as or better than they can.

A great manager delegates as much of the routine work as possible to their team. It has been said that 'real leadership is a when a leader makes it their goal to create more leaders'. It is the fostering of this leadership that makes a person successful.

Passing the buck when something goes wrong is a sure way to lose the respect of the group. It is quite common to hear a weak manager who is on the carpet publicly blame one of their employees for an error. Whose responsibility is it? A real leader is not afraid to admit their mistakes and does not lash out at others. In fact, people find it much more appealing when someone declares that he is not infallible.

Losing one's temper in front of others is a sure sign of weakness. A person must master themselves before he can effectively lead others. Losing your temper will lead to dissension and will turn your team against you rapidly.

You should not allow yourself or former friends to take special privileges. The new manager is sure to be criticized if he attempts to display their new-found pres-tige in this manner.

Leaning too much toward either management or employees is another common error in supervision. A line manager is the "middle-man" between top management and the employee, and a proper balance must be maintained in this relationship. This balance is so important to a new manager that we will discuss it in more detail.

"The Fine Line"

When an employee is first appointed to a manager position he must draw a fine line in their relationships between themselves and their employees. If he assumes a false dignity or attempts any show of authority, their employees will laugh at them behind their back. At the same time, the old "buddy-buddy" relationships, the close familiarities with fellow employees that were once enjoyed, are no longer appropriate. Drawing this line is one of the most difficult parts of the new job, but it must be done.

To maintain this balance, try asking the employees for advice or help rather than giving the impression that you know it all. Let the employees know that you have confidence in them, maintain a friendly but conservative attitude, treat everyone the same, be consistent, and set a good example.

If you follow the principles of good human relations, which will be covered later in this book, and if you will think of your job as a sacred trust and that you will carry out your duties in terms of what is best for the company, you will go very far.

Duties and responsibilities of management

An accurate list of duties and responsibilities can only be made in reference to a particular manager. However, the following list includes some of the typical duties and responsibilities common to most managers:

- Get the right employee on the job at the right time.

- Economical use and placement of materials.

- Attendance control (absence and tardiness).

- Accident prevention and control of hazards.

- Keeping the employees satisfied and happy.

- Addressing grievances.

- Maintaining discipline.

- Keeping records and making reports.

- Maintaining quality and quantity of work.

- Planning and scheduling of work.

- Training employees.

- Requisitioning tools, equipment, and materials.

- Inspection, care, and preservation of tools and equipment.

- Giving direction.

- Developing and maintaining cooperation with other departments or personnel.

- Checking and inspecting tools and raw materials.

- Settling differences among the employees.

- Promoting teamwork.

- Preparing and disseminating rules and regulations, organizational channels, procedures, etc.

- Maintaining good housekeeping on the job.

Primary duties

Analyzing this list, we find the following major duties and responsibilities common to all manager positions:

- Work Accomplishment

- Safety, Health, Physical Welfare of the Employee

- Development of Cooperation

- Development of Morale

- Training and Development of Subordinates

- Records and Reports

Be responsible for productivity

The responsibility of every manager is work output. Whether the job is in an office or not, the manager is paid to see that the work is achieved in a reasonable amount of time.

As a manager you have four primary objectives to achieve this:

- Organize or plan the work to get maximum output with minimum effort and confusion.

- Delegate as much of the responsibility and authority for the actual work to others as often as possible.

- Oversee the work to ensure that it is done properly while keeping a balance to not be overbearing.

- Create leaders and promote your employees' growth.

The real estimate of a manager's worth is based primarily on their ability to get out the work in a timely manner with the least resistance. However, as a word of caution, the drive for high output must not overshadow consideration for the human element. People are not machines, and the manager who treats them as such will find that no amount of pressure will permanently increase their rate of work, in fact, it will decline sharply. Use this tactic at your own peril as you'll soon earn the dreaded "Micro-Manager" title and then it will be "us versus them" within your team.

Safety, Health, Physical Welfare of the employee Safety and production go hand-in-hand. The safe way is typically the efficient way. An injured employee is a non-producer. Real managers preach safety to the employees and set an example by working safely themselves. Just as we were chil-dren, we watch others and learn by example.

Likewise, showing concern over the health and physical welfare of your employees will pay off in production. It will add to the worker's feeling of self-esteem, and their respect for you will increase accordingly. You will gain more power just by being respectful of others.

Create cooperation

This involves more than just the development of cooperation within the managerial group.

Cooperation is a three-way deal:

- Cooperation within one's own department.

- Cooperation with the upper management.

- Cooperation with other managers.

Some managers develop a tightly-knit "team" with excellent cooperation within their own groups; the great manager thinks in terms of what is best for all and shows their own willingness to cooperate with others. Often you can effect change by simply making friends and showing support for another person's initiatives.

Create morale

The "esprit-de-corps" of the department and the willingness of the people to work toward common goals depend to a great extent upon the leadership of the manager. Normally, a productive department will be found to be a department with "high morale".

Morale can be generated in many different ways; one way is to foster a feeling of camaraderie through an exercise known as "Team Building". These exercises normally entail pep talks, luncheons, or going out to a fun place to enjoy some of what life has to offer. Besides, we don't live to work, we work to live.

Even though this may sound like an unproductive waste of work time, taking your department out for a day of fun once in a while will ensure that your team will produce more than twice as much as a manager who takes a hard line approach to the work ethic. Since 80% of our time is spent at work, it needs to be enjoyable for everyone.

People have coined the phrase "Work Hard, Play Hard" and this phrase is shown to have great truth. If your employees are not enjoying their work, they will only produce at a minimum level. The simple fact is that if people are happy they will work harder for you!

Train and develop your employees

A great manager is invariably a good teacher. Much of the manager's job is a teaching job. A great manager sees there is at least one employee trained and ready to take the manager's place. When a manager can step away from the job to take leave, etc., and the job continues to run smoothly, it is a sure sign of good leadership. Do not be afraid to teach every phase of your own work to at least one or two subordinates, but be sure that the person you have as your lead while you are away is not one of your "favorites" or you will cause dissension during your absence.

It is also important to ensure that your team is getting adequate training in all aspects of their respective jobs. Most certainly your team's jobs will change over time; either the software, the processes, the procedures, or even certain laws may effect this change. In order for your employees to feel they are growing in their job, it is important to send them to specialized, skill-targeting training.

Records and reports

Most managers do not like this part of the job, yet records and reports are a vital part of the work. Make it a point to keep neat, accurate records and reports—and get the reports in on time! That paperwork may look like a waste of time to you, but some day you will realize how much your job depends on it.

If you think about it, when information needs to be presented to upper level management, and they need to ensure that their projects and programs are being completed and on track, it's very important to have properly constructed reports that include metrics or major objective status items. This will ensure both you and your supervisor can track the work being performed.

Undoubtedly, your own supervisor must compile a report to their management that can show how their own teams are performing as well, so the better you communicate upward, the more visible and up-to-date your entire organization can become.

Perform balanced supervision

A great manager needs to pay proper attention to each phase of the job. Some managers are so intent upon getting out production that they neglect safety or training, or their employee's needs. Some managers neglect records and reports, in contrast to other people who like the paperwork and who devote too much of their time to this responsibility.

Some managers become so concerned with the human element that they neglect the production, or they take the opposite approach and get bogged down in paperwork, so keep a good balance and ensure that each of your employees get a chance to contribute to the design of your metrics and reports. You'll be happier and the reports will most often be better. Don't be a fool, your employees normally want their team to look good and will help iron out those last minute errors.

All of us have "hobbies" in supervision, and we tend to ride these hobbies.

This practice is called "Unbalanced Supervision". Real leaders force themselves to put the proper emphasis on each of their responsibilities. This is called "Balanced Supervision".

To ensure you are spending time on the appropriate things, use a calendar or task tracking software and create alarms based on dates for accomplishing even repetitive tasks, this will keep you on track and ensure you're performing in a balanced way.

CHAPTER SUMMARY

In this chapter, we've learned about the importance of management responsibilities, how to properly integrate yourself during your first day on the job, and what areas you'll typically be responsible for in your new management duties.

2

Traits of Leadership

CHAPTER OBJECTIVES:

- Study some of the traits which are desirable in company managers
- Learn how to develop leadership traits

The desirable traits of leadership

(OTHER THAN TECHNICAL KNOWLEGE)

If we would ask either top management officials or the employees themselves what traits they want in their managers, we would likely get long and varied list of attributes. However, the following considerations seem to be generally agreed upone. Of great importance to you is the fact that an employee may only be missing one of these traits but that one may be their downfall and I encourage you to extend as much aid to them as possible.

Loyalty

Loyalty is considered by many to be one of the most essential factors of leadership. Many experienced administrators and managers say that they would rather have a loyal employee who is not such an excellent performer than and non-loyal one who is otherwise excellent. Loyalties to the company, to the department, to the boss, to the people who work for you and with you; these are prerequisites of leadership. Loyalty begets loyalty. The surest way to get the respect and loyalty of your employees is to be loyal to them.

Every time you feel inclined to criticize management or your employees, stop doing that right away. You are "management" to your employees, and if you are not loyal, how can you expect loyalty from them? Be loyal first, if you aspire to lead others. If you are not showing loyalty, employees may assume that all management is not loyal to the company! Remember, you represent "Them" and "They" that employees refer to when speaking about their management staff.

Positive thinking

Many people can be classified into two types:

- *Positive Thinkers*

- *Negative Thinkers*

Real leaders will always be positive thinkers. They think in terms of how things can be done, not why they can't. They maintain an open mind to changes, new ideas, and training opportunities. They listen carefully to the other employees, not with the intention of opposing everything another says, but for the purpose of exploring the good ideas he or she presents.

Positive thinkers see some good in everyone and everything. They are enthusiastic about their jobs and the part they play in the company. Positive thinking helped accomplish almost everything worthwhile that has ever been accomplished in this world. If you want to lead others, start today by practicing the art of positive thinking.

Enjoyment of people

Have you ever met a really great leader—a top executive in a corporation, a fore-man of a huge industrial shop, a great artist, a bank president, a key man in gov-ernment? If so you probably received quite a shock! Likely as not, instead of the cold, aloof "man in an ivory tower" you expected, he turned out to be a mild mannered, humble, friendly, plain old human being! As a matter of fact you probably began to wonder how he ever attained such a position! He made you feel important too, by their warm welcome, their close attention to your words, their interest in what you were doing, and their questions asking for your opinions.

Such leaders long ago learned the value of making the fellow employee feel important, instead of trying to show their own importance. They learned that people hunger for appreciation and that others will work willingly for the manager who likes and understands them.

Being approachable

They take time to see and hear their employees. For this kind of manager, employees often remark that he or she is "so easy to talk to." The first step a new manager should take is to get to know your employees personally. Try and keep an open mind and don't let yourself judge them. Everyone is different, and not everyone will be exactly the way you want them to be.

IMAGINE A SIGN AROUND THE NECK OF EVERY PERSON YOU MEET. THAT SIGN READS: "I WANT TO FEEL IMPORTANT."

A manager, who makes a hobby of studying human nature and who lives to help others, not only finds their job more pleasant, but also creates followers too!

The cornerstone of human relations is a genuine interest in—and liking for—people, and the ability to empathize with their own needs and wants in life.

Showing Initiative

Initiative is the evidence of an open and alert mind. The person with initiative continually looks for better ways to do things instead of waiting for someone else to do it. He doesn't put off until tomorrow what should be done today. If an unsafe condition is observed, action is taken to correct it before something bad happens. If there is a human relations problem within the group, positive action is taken to straighten it out. If equipment needs repairs or replacement, a manager with initiative will repair or replace it. If it's noticed that a new form or procedure would simplify the job, he will outline this new form of procedure and ask the team if it sounds good. If he sees an inadequacy in himself, he takes action to overcome it.

Weak people will not do more than just the bare minimum of work. The person who is afraid to do more than what their salary calls for seldom has much salary to call for! Leaders are not afraid to take on more work than they are paid for—such action often leads to increased knowledge of the job and higher positions. You should recognize when you have one of these leaders and value them greatly because they will more than likely be your best employees.

Being Decisive

Leaders are able to make decisions. One of the most common complaints heard from employees is this: "You can't get a decision out of him". A great number of the decisions that have to be made by managers are on petty things. As often as not, the employee merely wants the manager's approval on some minor action where he already knows what should be done. A prompt "yes" from the manager is all that is necessary. In many minor decisions, it makes little difference whether the answer is "yes" or "no". The important thing is to get the answer.

The manager who stalls, puts off, evades, or downright refuses to give a decision is a real bottleneck. This is also a signal to an employee that he is not being taken seriously and that their issues are not important, so be careful when rejecting an employee after he has approached you with some of these questions.

Of course, there are times when a decision requires careful consideration of many factors and much deliberation. In such cases, tell the employee when to return for the decision and see to it that the decision is ready when promised.

Being Fair

Employees are extremely sensitive to partiality by the manager. They will even pick on little things where there was no intention of favoritism on the part of the manager. The great manager must think ahead on changes made, decisions handed down, work assigned, pay raises, promotions, etc.

In each instance you must ask yourself: "My choice will make this person happy, but how will every other individual in my department feel about it?" If you don't know the answer to this question, you should get feedback privately from each of the members of your team. The best way to approach this is to ask them who they think ought to be promoted, or get general feedback from each person.

It is particularly hard for new managers to avoid favoritism with old buddies among their former co-workers. Some managers can tell you of cases where they were too friendly with certain employees; then the time came for disciplinary action and it was very difficult to administer, as can readily be seen.

Great managers will also warn against over-familiarity off the job with a certain few of the employees. Other employees view such activity with suspicion, and morale within the department will consequently lower.

Showing Sincerity and integrity

Managers who deal with their employees squarely and honestly all the time win and hold the respect of others. They talk to their employees on a "person-to-per-son basis". They are not afraid to face the facts and say what they think is necessary. But don't go over the line and say detrimental things, it's usually best to approach someone lightly and respectfully and offer him or her guidance and support, not direct attacks.

Being Consistent

Consistency of thought and action are important if the employees are going to know where they stand. Being too strict one day, too lax the next, is worse than being consistently strict or consistently lax. Openly exhibiting a wide range of moods is not good. Strike a happy medium between firmness and laxness and be consistent. If you find yourself getting upset, take a walk or read calmly to take your mind off things.

Being Dependable

Dependability is one of the marks of true integrity. Dependability involves meeting your obligations promptly. A reputation for being a "square-shooter" is worth every effort on your part. This reputation must be built early, even prior to your appointment as manager. One violation of integrity may take months to rectify, if it's even possible at all.

Being Aggressive

Leaders must have the drive and will-power to do things. They also must have a hunger to be somebody, a will to get ahead. However, this zeal and enthusiasm must be controlled to the extent that others are not irritated by your drive.

The tactful leader is quietly aggressive, gently pushing for what he wants without being obvious about it. People are wary and resentful of the person who pushes too hard. They do not like to be driven. They resist change. They also resent the person who too obviously pushes for promotion or is too forceful in general.

Showing Humility

People will be more comfortable in your presence when they see that you also are human and imperfect. Real leaders have learned the knack of being human on the job. Weak managers cover up their feelings of inferiority by setting up a barrier between themselves and their employees, by a show of authority, by maintaining a "big front", or by assumption of a false dignity.

Real leaders realize that others can do things just as well or better than they; that others are just as intelligent as or more intelligent than they. "Every person is in some way superior". With this viewpoint, you cannot help but improve your human relations and realize that each and every person has qualities that can undoubtedly be used for the benefit of the team.

Displaying self-confidence

Great managers have a quiet confidence (not an arrogant or cocky confidence) based on thorough knowledge of the job and belief in their own abilities. Confidence begets confidence. The mousy, hesitant manager who lacks confidence in themselves cannot inspire confidence in their employees and can easily make them uncomfortable and resentful.

Be a teacher

A great part of the manager's job consists of instructing the employees in one way or another. Even the giving of orders is a form of instruction. Every manager should learn and practice the art of good public speaking, the principles of on-the-job instruction.

The person who cannot stand and express ideas to one or a group of people should not be a manager. The company must have people in managerial positions that can train and develop others.

Be friendly

We like to work for the person who looks at everything in a friendly manner.

Ready smiles, a friendly approach, will open doors like magic. Many of the daily problems on the job would easily be solved if everyone took a friendly approach to them.

The stern, forbidding manner has no place in modern supervision. Friendliness is contagious, and the friendly boss has a friendly group. The real leader is business-like, but he looks at things in a friendly fashion. How much more pleasant it is to work in a place where everyone is friendly? Many people will work for less money to stay with a friendly manager.

Some unenlightened managers take their job too seriously. They will fight at the drop of a hat on any issue, even if the outcome of that conflict is insignificant.

Great managers maintain a consistently friendly attitude, even when they do not feel that way inside. They avoid criticizing. Instead they try to see the good points of each person. Remember that people hunger for praise, and sincere praise from the boss is one of the most powerful stimulants to production known! And it costs so little!

To develop a friendly personality, try the following suggestions:

• Be conscious of the other person and note what they do. Talk about subjects that interest them and they will think of you as someone with an interesting personality. Forget yourself through an active interest in other people.

• Assume that people like you. If you show that you want people to talk to you, they will respond warmly. On the other hand, if you act in a reserved, reclusive manner, people will assume that you wish to be left alone. If you give the impression that you enjoy your own company more than the company of others, they will let you have yourself to yourself.

• When you greet a person, greet him emphatically. Don't mumble "good morning" from the corner of your mouth as you concentrate on pouring yourself a cup of coffee. Smile, look that person in the eye, and say "GOOD MORNING!" If you're out of handshake range, give a short wave. If you feel fake during your first attempt to be cordial, just continue practicing until it feels genuine.

• Build up the other person's feelings of self-worth. Note things about which the person feels inferior. Offer this person sincere compliments that suggest their qualities are greater than what he believes them to be. Do not talk about him, but compliment them on their intelligent acts. But be sure to avoid cliché remarks, as these will only sound hollow and insincere.

- Admit your own defects. You need not deliberately make a monkey of yourself but when you have acted as one let others make humorous remarks at your expense. It takes confidence and security to wear a genuine smile as you endure a little ribbing at your own expense.

- Practice the use of the word "You" and avoid "I". One measure of your personality is the number of times you say, "you", "your", "he", "his", "she", and "her", rather than "I", "me", "my", or "mine". The test of your social skills is not the number of ideas that you give others, but rather how many ideas you get from them.

CHAPTER SUMMARY

In this chapter, we focused on which traits of leadership allow a person to progress into management and the effect these traits may have on your own performance as a manager. Not everyone will have all these traits so the goal is not to be perfect, but to be aware of the traits that you must foster in order to improve yourself and be the great manager that you want to be.

3

Maintaining Discipline

CHAPTER OBJECTIVES:

- Learn how to give orders

- Learn how to reprimand properly

- Learn how to achieve positive discipline rather than negative discipline

- Study the human relations aspects of the discipline problem

How to provide direction

Most disciplinary actions are the result of an employee's failure to carry out an assigned task. Therefore, it goes to show that a great manager should give a lot of thought to providing proper direction.

Common orders:

- The Command. "DO THIS!"

- The Request. "Will you do this?" or "Can you do this?"

- The Suggestion (This usually works the best) "Would it be a good idea to try this?" or "Do you have any thoughts on how this can be done?"

- The Volunteer "Who would like to do this?" or "I'd like to have three people for this job."

Use of orders

(The Conditions under which the order is given)

- **THE DIRECT COMMAND** should be used when there is immediate danger; a fire, an accident or other emergency, disobedience of safety rules, etc.

- **THE SIMPLE REQUEST** is the best type of order to give for daily tasks.
  This method is used for most orders given by great managers.

- **THE SUGGESTION** is excellent in situations where you wish to have an employee go on their own, or when you do not have time to work out the details, or where you do not know exactly how the job should be done.
  This is usually the most effective method because it solves the issue for the employee and for you. This method builds confidence and morale with your employee and also shows the employee that you have confidence in him. However, it is not always clear-cut, and you certainly would have no recourse if the job were not done properly.

- **THE VOLUNTEER METHOD** is used for disagreeable, dirty jobs. It is good for those little extra jobs that often come up. It can also be used for those little routine jobs, if not used to excess.

Consider the individual

(The personality of the employee must be considered.)

- **THE DIRECT COMMAND** might have to be used in giving even routine orders to the careless, lazy, insubordinate, or thick-skulled individual.
  It is normally reserved for those to whom we must speak firmly and positively, except for the unusual situations we talked about on the last page.

- **THE REQUEST** is by far the best type of order to use with normal employees. With most employees a simple request in the form of a question has the full effect of a direct order, but it does not irritate them.
  Instead it fosters a feeling of cooperative effort, or teamwork. It makes the person believe that you are on their side and he is not doing it for you; he will feel he is doing the task for himself.

- **THE SUGGESTION** is excellent for those to whom a suggestion or hint is sufficient. Employees with real initiative like to be "put on their own."
  With sensitive, highly intelligent individuals a mere hint that something is desired is enough to get them started. The suggestion type of order puts the "bee" on the employee to show what he can do.

- **THE VOLUNTEER METHOD** of giving orders has its place where difficult, dirty, disagreeable, or extra jobs must be done. This technique is also very helpful when changing someone's job slightly; giving them the opportunity to speak about the change and feel they are a part of the change. The only problem with this is the "eager beavers" will volunteer, which means that a certain few will be doing all of these jobs. Some people are reticent or bashful and do not like to "stick their necks out". They will resent the "eager beavers" who may appear to be "polishing the apple". At the same time, the volunteers may get tired of doing all the tough jobs. Therefore, the volunteer method should not be used excessively.

Elements of an order

Whether verbal or written, every directive should contain the answers to the following questions, unless you know that they are already clearly understood by the employee:

- Who?

- What?

- When?

- Where?

- How?

- Why?

Important Note: Remember, explaining "why" is one of the most important things to include in a directive. Keep in mind that you as a manager often have more information than the employee. Sometimes that lack of knowledge can eat at an employee badly enough to cause problems in both performance and morale, and can even rub off on other groups or individuals.

Provide tasks

- Clearly

- Completely

- Concisely

- Confidently

- Correctly

Take precautions

• Be sure that the task is necessary—avoid superfluous orders.

• Be sure that you have sufficient authority to assign the task.

• Be brief and specific.

• Fit the order to the individual and the situation.

• If important, have the employee repeat the order or write it down.

Follow up no matter how clearly a task is given. You can never be too sure that the employee completely understands it. And don't be too judgmental over a lack of understanding; your job is guidance not perfection. Therefore, follow-up is necessary. However, watch how you follow-up your tasks. Much resentment may be raised if this is done carelessly or too often. If done too often will be viewed as mistrust or micro-management. The follow-up may be done by actual inspection (not in a snooping manner) or by an indirect approach like this:

"Juanita, would you like any help on that job?" or, "Cliff, did you have any trouble on that report?" (Note the assumption that they are carrying out the task).

The reprimand

When a task is disobeyed or not carried out, the manager would be remiss in their duties if they did not do something about it. The most common type of discipline used by managers is the simple reprimand.

1. The reprimand must be fitted to the individual and the situation. A innocently misspoken word will be more crushing to the sensitive individual than the tongue-lashing you might give the more thick-skinned person.

2. The reprimand should be a calm, constructive action—not a destructive function. You are interested in building a good employee, not tearing them down. You should be interested in the underlying causes, not in how to get even with the employee.

3. Failure to reprimand when it is due is also bad. No one likes the manager who is too soft and ingratiating. If one employee gets by with something, the manager may lose control. Too many reprimands are just as bad and will lead to dissention.

The primary components of discipline

- Fairness

- Firmness

- Friendliness

Reprimand procedure

1. Get all the facts!

2. Reprimand in PRIVATE!—Never in front of others!

3. Put the employee at ease—Give a word of praise first, if appropriate, to take out the sting.

4. Use no sarcasm, anger, or abuse.

5. Fit the reprimand to the individual.

6. Lay out all the facts.

7. Have all the facts at hand in case the employee attempts to deny the charge.

8. Ask why the person did it.

9. Try to get the employee to admit their mistake.

10. Don't threaten. (They know how far you can go.)

11. Once there is an admission of being wrong, the reprimand is over.

12. Leave on a friendly note; let him know the incident is closed.

13. Later follow up with casual and friendly contact.

Important reminders:

- You must get along with the employee in the future.

- You must keep them as a working, producing department.

- You must be able to get along with your own conscience!

- Don't make enemies within your team

Positive and negative discipline

More severe disciplinary actions include warnings, suspensions, and removals. All of these are serious. The manager should never threaten an employee with the use of these actions, since the approval of a higher authority will most likely be required in each case.

So far we have talked of discipline in terms of punishment. Actually, discipline is much more than a reprisal for wrongdoing. Discipline exists in a positive manner where no disciplinary actions ever have to be taken. Most people realize they cannot exist in nature or in a job without self-discipline. No organization can function and no progress can be made unless individuals conform to what is best for the whole group.

Important Note: The manager who can build team spirit and cooperation will have no real discipline problem!

Positive discipline

The trend in discipline which is being widely studied by intelligent executives and managers is the force that stems from within the individual which prompts them to obey the rules and regulations.

People in most organizations do what is right because they do not want to hurt the group as a whole; because they believe that by following the accepted rules they will more quickly (and safely) accomplish their objectives. The manager that has built up this team spirit has few discipline problems. Only in very rare instances does the manager have to resort to negative discipline.

Negative discipline

Negative discipline was the only kind of discipline in the old days, still practiced by the dictator-type of manager. It is discipline based on fear and the threat of punishment. This type of discipline stems from one's desires to dominate by force. One of the issues with this form of management is that an employee subjected to this type of discipline will do only enough to get by when you are watching!

When you leave for even a few minutes, discipline and work ethic fly out the window! The employee's only motive to work is developed from fear of reprisal.

This can severely undermine progression within an organization by reducing output to only that which is necessary rather than to exceed expectations.

Employees will typically avoid doing any type of work that presents risk to them. Keep in mind, the most progressive, productive, and innovative work is accomplished when an employee extends their risks beyond what is necessary to get the job done, so it is important to avoid control-by-fear as it will have the effect of stifling this creativity and productivity even with others in the group who aren't directly subjected to your "wrath".

Effectiveness test

Ask yourself the question: Did it build morale? If it did, then your reprimand was successfully executed.

Human relations aspect of discipline

The human relationship which exists between the manager and their employees is usually an indication that the manager appreciates and understands their employees; that they have the employee's interest and welfare at heart, and that they respect their employee's opinions, knowledge, and skill.

Human relations components

What leads to positive discipline?

1. The great manager understands the principles, standards, rules, and regulations necessary for good conduct, and believes in these things and practices it themselves.

2. The great manager knows their people as individuals, and treats them fairly and impartially.

3. The great manager has developed a sense of "belonging" in the group.They have also developed a sense of security and trust within the team.

4. The great manager gets information through proper channels to their group, and promptly eliminates rumors.

5. The great manager uses their authority sparingly and always without displaying it.

6. The great manager has learned to delegate authority as far down the line as possible.

7. The great manager never makes issues out of minor infractions, nor do they make personal issues out of disciplinary matters.

8. The great manager must display confidence in the group, rather than suspicion; employees are reluctant to betray expressed confidence.

9. The great manager has trained their group technically.

10. The great manager has given care to the mental and physical welfare of the group.

11. The great manager has tried to avoid errors, but has shown willingness to admit errors when made.

12. The great manager has developed loyalty within the group and for the group.

13. The great manager knows that idle hands or minds lead to trouble, so they keep them busy. Slack work periods can be used for training or mentoring.

14. The great manager knows that discipline cannot be routine due to individual differences.

Primary causes of misconduct:

- Discontent

- Idling

- Lack of interest

- Misunderstanding the rules or regulations

- Lack of enforcement or accountability

- Resentment or emotional strain

These are only some of the principal causes of misconduct. The wise manager will avoid the necessity for formal discipline by removing such causes.

Chapter summary

In this chapter, we've learned the value of knowing how to give direction to your group and get them focused on tasks without creating resentment or annoyance.

We've learned the proper way to reprimand if we feel it is necessary, and we've also shared some insight on the human relations aspect of managing people.

4

Developing Cooperation

CHAPTER OBJECTIVES:

- Explain the meaning of cooperation and its significance to you as a great manager

- Study some of the basic elements of group psychology

- Study some of the ways in which the manager can achieve total "vertical" and "horizontal" cooperation of all parties

Cooperation

The cooperation challenge

In today's world, since we are fast-paced and things change at alarming rates, it has become more important to be able to quickly and completely get the cooperation of others. You must do everything that you can to understand and practice the principles in this chapter, as they will change the way that you conduct yourself with your group.

In your company, as with any organization, productivity is paramount and is only accomplished through the efforts of many people cooperating harmoniously. Your company must strive to find managers that have the finesse and desire to get the willing cooperation of their employees.

In the workplace, employees will produce just to the extent that they feel like producing. This will is based on the manager's ability to win their group's cooperation and trust. The truest measure of a manager's leadership is the ability to get good cooperation between members of the team as well as others. Cooperation, in return, is the reflection of the group's trust, devotion, and respect towards their manager. This means that cooperation must be based on the principles of good human relations and compassion for the employee.

People are for the most part naturally cooperative if they are given the chance to prove themselves. Keep in mind the competition that each of them is up against, and realize this can cause issues. The most common issue is jealousy, which can lead to slowed productivity and problems within the group. This is a sign of poor leadership, and must be corrected quickly.

Your cooperative commitment

Great managers remain committed to fostering cooperation and ensuring that their department sees that they are also cooperative with others. A great manager must remain cooperative with other managers and their team in order to create an environment where this can flourish. This is called "Vertical" and "Horizontal" cooperation.

- **VERTICAL** cooperation applies to a manager's relationship with his superiors above and subordinates below.

- **HORIZONTAL** cooperation applies to the relationship with peers, management staff, and the subordinates of other departments.

Psychology of Cooperation

Basic components of group psychology

Every great manager should understand the dynamic that occurs in order to achieve cohesion within a group and the things necessary to achieve cohesion:

- A Feeling of "Security" in their job

- A feeling of "Belonging" to the department

- A feeling of "being important" to the success of the team

- A feeling of pride in the department

- A feeling of accomplishment by the department toward attainment of common goals

- A feeling of recognition from outside the department

- A feeling of personal satisfaction with their own needs be it pay, advancement, education, etc.

When these 7 things remain in balance, the team will foster high output, ingenuity, and satisfaction from all the employees both inside and outside the department. Once a new member joins your department, they will soon be enchanted by this dynamic and will personally identify themselves as part of the department. The job will become part of them in an essential and personal way. The more employees feel they are part of the department, the more it will create an extremely successful organization with the ability to execute with speed and accuracy.

Things a great manager must do to create this type of environment are:

- Provide goals for the group that is created by the group

- Provide some sort of reward, whether it is psychological or otherwise to the members of the department

Cooperation failures

When entering any department, you can almost feel the sensation in the air. It's quite easy to tell when a group lacks the ability to efficiently cooperate with each other. Their work areas usually depict how they feel within their department. You may even be able to tell by the looks on their faces, or how you are greeted. It may be obvious based on how their work looks.

Poor cooperation can be identified by:

- Jealousy

- Friction

- Bickering

- Frequent accidents

- Sloppy work

- Grievances

- Absenteeism

- Criticism of management

- High turnover

- Poor planning

- Lack of training or indifference to it

In an environment such as this, it is easy to see what the output of the department will be (poor!) and how it will affect the company (badly!).

This is usually a good sign that a manager is not doing an effective job or may be taking on too many other tasks to do an effective job. It is important that we create and foster a good working environment so that our employees will produce to their maximum output capacity.

Elements to consider

Fostering cooperation within your department is largely based on your ability to adapt your own behaviors to meet the environment and the changes taking place within it. You must go out of your way to show that you are willing to cooperate so as to lead by example. You can't just command your employees to be cooperative; this is an art form, and must be practiced as such.

Resistance to change

Everyone resists change. This is evident in all our lives every day and everywhere. People are creatures of the routine. I know, because I myself have a routine. Every morning, I get up, get a cup of coffee, sit on my couch, and watch my favorite show or the morning news. If for some reason, I must break with this routine, I feel disappointed and frustrated, and the rest of my day can go by significantly hindered until I can get myself "re-aligned" to the work that must be accomplished.

At work, I've noticed that even when things change for the better, people have a hard time with it. Many people give off vibes of distaste, disgust, and general negativity whenever something that has been done in a certain way for any length of time changes; even if it's good for them. Change is difficult!

There are a few small reminders to take into account whenever you want to enact change within your group. The following suggestions may help:

- Make changes slowly whenever possible

- Carefully time any changes

- Consider the group's mentality and feelings before moving forward

- Changes should be agreed upon by the group before they are made

Changes can be made using very subtle hints to multiple members of your team who can then lead your group to make the changes themselves The best approach to getting change accepted is to convene a meeting with the group, suggest the changes necessary, ask for suggestions, and make the appropriate changes that are necessary. This methodology will lead your team down the best path and most likely, with input from the team, you may discover things that may not have otherwise occurred to you.

At the end of the day, the team has to agree on what needs to be done. Without taking these important steps, the change will never actually flourish and be accepted by the team. Managers who don't learn the act of delegating decisions as well as work will develop an uncooperative and very apathetic team. Change is an important part of any organization, but must be done in the right way to foster acceptance.

Principle of exception

The exception principle is very important technique in today's management tool-box. This principle is where a team and a manager try to create simple routines or repeatable processes within their group's area of responsibility. This promotes efficiency and the ability to adapt quickly when the business environment changes. If your group functions using simplified routines rather than complex, time-consuming tasks, you will find yourself only having to handle the exceptions of the routines, which will greatly enhance your ability to manage a larger department without constant supervision. One concept that is surprisingly important is delegating the act of "final inspection" or a peer review on your group's final deliverables rather than having every deliverable reviewed by you, the manager. This will reduce delivery times for your group, and ensure your production maintains smooth scalability. Developing the ability to delegate tasks is one of the most important steps to becoming a great manager. Keep in mind, the productivity of your group is reviewed by your upper management and you don't want yourself to become a roadblock to that success. Your success and the perception of your group directly reflect how your peers and your management view you.

Communication

Communicate on a regular basis with your team. It is of the utmost importance that your team understands what is going on, and why changes are occurring.

Remember, each of them must keep a clear vision of the group's current goals to attain success, and without proper communication as to why changes are needed and why they are good, an employee can get lost within their own fears and doubts rather than promoting harmony within the group and the company. This also allows the team to provide essential feedback for your decision-making.

Whenever communicating changes try and refrain from making comments that reflect badly on the company or its upper management. Any of these comments could discourage your employees from being productive, even though they may relate to your comment, it's best left un-spoken. Besides, your team is in no position to take action on your own grievances and they can lower morale and productivity. They are best pointed out to upper management, since it is your management's job to work hard to assist you in any grievances that you have with decisions they make.

Developing the group

In today's challenging world, the manager who trains his employees will earn a good reputation by reassuring them that they are important to the overall success of the team. As we said before, don't be afraid to train an employee beyond your own capabilities; besides, someday you may want to take another job, or move on to another company and you'll need someone to replace you.

You must show interest in your department's training goals and you must work hard to ensure the group learns on a constant basis. This allows the group to feel advancement even when they are not yet being promoted or if there is no opportunity for promotion. By doing this, you will ensure cooperation and loyalty. "The single greatest contribution a manager can make is to develop the people they lead in a positive way".

Output restriction

We now know that internally, to a team, it is not uncommon for team members to warn each other when someone seems to be "pushing the envelope" or working too hard. This is common for a group to go through as no one wants to be viewed as not working hard enough, or to be compared to another "outperforming" person in the group. Many times your group may resort to name-calling or ridicule of the person to bring them back to the "normal" work pace.

A great manager must be careful when making the attempt to increase work rates or set "quotas" of production. You must also be careful of increasing competition too much. It is better to approach these issues by winning the support of the team with regard to increasing their productivity or you will cause resentment towards you or among team members. Try not to compare these high-output individuals to others in the group or you will create resentment and your efforts to increase output will backfire. Be careful to distribute the workload evenly and not favor one employee over another.

Favoritism

Everyone resents favoritism both on and off the job. A great manager draws the line between themselves and their employees and does not allow themselves to appear as though they are favoring one employee over another. I know this is a very difficult task and unnatural for most people, but it will do you well to heed this advice.

Your participation in social activities is a great contribution to your team, but you should remember that you are held higher than others, and that your involvement must include everyone or you will create resentment in your team members. Concentrate on creating harmony by ensuring that everyone is welcome to any event that you decide to attend which includes employees in your group.

Set the example

The great manager who is enthusiastic about the job and is friendly with his team but does not use fear, uncertainty, and doubt to accomplish their goals, and who does not use abuse or threats to attain the lead does a lot to create cooperation and respect in his own group by example of their own actions.

Learn to give credit

Great managers look for every possible way to give credit for the work performed to the people in their organization. This is a key factor in the development of cooperation because it can make others feel good about what they are doing.

When people are recognized by their management it creates a sense of pride in their work which will propel them to do even better work and productivity will increase tremendously. In fact, most of the greatest leaders in our country were quick to ensure that they pass on credit to others rather than keeping it for themselves.

In most cultures it is a great sign of strength as well as humility to give credit to others. Leaders that are humble are more likely to be trusted because they are not viewed as egotists. If your team views you that way, it can be very counterproductive and it's certainly not the perception you want others to have of you. People are quick to mistrust anyone who appears to only be concerned with their own glory and ego.

Handling personal affairs

Personal problems are very common throughout each day in the work environment. The great manager must address these issues without prejudice and with due care. Rumors, disputes, or family troubles will enter the lives of your employees at one time or another. These issues can obviously cause a major disruption in your department.

The most common mistake is to discount the employee's feelings and ignore the issue which leads the employee to feel that you are not sympathetic towards them; this is certainly the wrong approach to have. The best thing to do in these situations is to offer good, wholesome advice and positive support. Remember, these are people you must work with, and they have emotions that you must acknowledge even if you are not really sympathetic to their issues.

In every instance you should do the following: listen, gather the facts, sympathize, and then tactfully bring about a solution so that the group can get back to work harmoniously. If the issues are work related, such as disputes between employees, you should confront these issues one-on-one with the person or persons involved (privately of course) and then try to solve them quickly before the issue gets out of hand and the group gets damaged by it.

Cooperation and your superiors

One of the most important people in your career is your own supervisor. This person holds the keys to your success or demise in the role you play. Whether or not you personally like that person, you must get along with them. Sometimes, if you cannot get along, you must decide for yourself whether or not it's time to move on to another position where you can.

This is a tough position to be in; the most important thing you must do is be honest with your own supervisor; people are far more understanding when they believe you are being straight and honest with them.

Loyalty

Loyalty is an important aspect of human relations, it is very important that you remain loyal to your supervisor. Most managers agree that the most important aspect of one's work is loyalty to management. A loyal person does not offer criticism of their own superiors, as it communicates dissention to your employees and will foster an environment of mistrust.

When the heat is on, you must ensure that you defend your management as a loyal person. Keep in mind, loyalty does not extend to defending them against illegal actions. If anyone asks you to perform illegal acts, it must be reported to your Human Resources or Ethics department immediately, don't be a fool. But loyalty does mean that you should stand by your management whenever the lines are drawn, a united front is an unbeatable army.

Disloyalty will backfire for you in several ways. First, more often than not, your management will find out about any disloyalties that are being played against them, so this will not bode well for you. And second, because of this, you will more than likely be passed up and left behind without ever knowing why. A disloyal manager cannot expect loyalty from their own employees; in fact it will create disloyalty throughout the group.

Dependability

Another very important aspect in the relationship with your own management is to ensure that you are dependable. There are many ways to be dependable such as arriving at work on time, completing your work on time, and continuing to improve your skills to do better work.

It's quite annoying to others when someone always has excuses, and never finishes anything that has been promised. Now, of course there are always some exceptions to this and valid reasons for delays, but generally these are more often caused by factors outside of your control, and you should be able to distinguish the difference between these.

No one is perfect, so don't expect it, but you should expect some level of consistency. Actually, when you see an employee whose behavior or productivity is inconsistent, you should sit down with them, and, instead of issuing a reprimand, voice the observation that they seem to be falling behind and make the offer to help. More often than not there is an issue they need your help with.

A great manager needs employees who are not afraid to share their thoughts or objections to his ideas. In fact, the best ideas come from within the group, so listen respectfully. If you have someone who constantly disagrees this can be a problem that may need to be dealt with privately. A great manager is neither afraid nor defensive when employees suggest or point out that they are wrong.

Let pride rest on your shoulders, not in your head, you'll find this a very good way of rounding up creative spirit in your group. If people feel they cannot express their opinions, you may not hear the idea destined to create that next big money maker for the company, or you may lose the opportunity to grow and learn from current mistakes!

The light suggestion

Many managers don't like outspoken or blunt people. It's very common to get frustrated by people that have this trait. Don't fret, as sometimes it's good to hear feedback. If you have an outspoken person, use them to your group's advantage, but guide them with one-on-one talks.

First, you must ensure that you are on speaking terms and, whenever making a point to meet with your employees, take a teaching/mentoring approach rather than a scolding approach. You should guide them to make suggestions by phrasing them as a question. The same holds true when you speak with your own management. When speaking with your management, make suggestions using a question.

A good example of a light suggestion might be "What do you think if we do this …" or "Have you thought about this …?" This allows your own manager to mentally consider his response without feeling attacked or pressured. If your manager feels pressured, he might respond by getting defensive and taking an opposing view simply because he feels threatened by your approach. The light suggestion is a very tactful way of presenting new information and is much more easily digested by the human mind.

Keep that in mind whenever you have creative thoughts. Take notes, write them out, and consider the different angles that may be pertinent to your idea. This way you can carefully plan the suggestion, and be more informed when you approach your management. The goal is to make your management a better decision-maker rather than having to think too hard about it, and therefore you will be looked at as a well-informed person who does their homework without making short-sighted decisions. Be prepared to take the idea to your manager with the solution already well-planned, this allows them to make informed decisions, and will ultimately result in your ideas being implemented.

There will come a time when your management will give you some work to do that you really don't feel is appropriate or, worse, you're convinced it's a mistake. You can approach them and suggest an alternate solution without asserting that they're "wrong". The power of suggestion can change a person's opinion dramatically. But if they insist, don't argue with them. Pick your battles wisely based on the person you are dealing with and the surrounding issues and concerns you are already aware of.

Keep management informed

Every manager likes to know what is going on in their team, so it is very important that you ensure your management knows the important things. Keep in mind that they have many people's needs to attend to and that even though many would love to hear your story, they simply don't have the time to hear every detail.

It's best to keep them advised of employee issues, staffing issues, and serious mistakes, but don't bother them with superfluous detail. Even though it may be tempting to show off your talent for "telling a good story", you will only inspire them to avoid you when they see you coming. They actually feel more comfortable simply knowing that you are handling it.

Don't let an important, serious issue bake in the oven. Ensure that any major issues are discussed immediately with your management so that they are not blindsided by someone from another part of the organization. This way they can remain calm, and formulate a good decision or action plan to remediate the problem.

Being un-informed when a major issue is at hand is quite embarrassing to management. However it is important that you understand that this may still happen from time to time and you must be prepared to help your management when this occurs.

Don't be such a baby.
Competition in the workplace
is good for everybody.

Foster group-to-group competition

Often, there is fierce competition fostered within some groups. Poorly handled, this can lead to friction, jealousy, and spite. You should ensure that this good clean competition does not prevent you from cooperating with managers of other departments. It is a very important duty to ensure your employees are working competitively with other groups, but in cooperation with their peers while observing any obvious organizational boundaries or functional coverage areas.

You should make every effort to do everything you can for another department and show that you are all on the same team. If you show a willingness to cooperate and provide people and knowledge to them whenever you can, this will avoid any issues of the "us versus them" type of attitudes. If you don't, they may make it very difficult for you to achieve your goals, and can be counterproductive to the company's success.

Avoid overlapping authority

In large organizations different departments can sometimes have similar or overlapping functions. This is not always bad, but it can be because it has the potential to cause animosity or fear. The best approach when dealing with these sorts of issues is to quickly team up with the management that has the similar priorities and decide "one-on-one" who should do what, and correct any issues diplomatically so that you may co-exist and deliver for the organization appropriately. Don't let issues fester and go to upper management unless of course all options are exhausted.

An important duty of a manager is to ensure this overlap does not happen. You should be careful and consider the ramifications of assigning duties so that other members of management do not see you as a threat, nor are you assigning similar tasks which are already handled in a different part of the organization. This would be seriously counterproductive to you and your goals of providing good and efficient service to your organization.

When dealing with other employees in other departments, you should never overstep your authority to provide direction. Make sure of this each time you need direct cooperation with another department. You must ensure their management is aware of the interaction and that you are not trying to encroach on their "turf" or realms of direct influence. Remember, this is a territorial game, and you are in competition with these folks, even if you don't see it.

Don't criticize other managers

Each time you find yourself beginning to criticize other managers, please stop! Don't get caught up in this sort of behavior. This leads your team to mistrust management, and not believe in the company as a whole. This will begin to degrade employee morale and the cooperative attitude that you must have in order to be successful. Your comments could also be leaked to the other organization or department with whom you are trying hard to get cooperation from. This can lead you down a really difficult path. You may find yourself pigeon-holed quickly if the other organization has more clout.

Often, talking badly about other people makes your subordinates believe that you'll talk badly about them, and leads them to distrust you and stray from your goals. Be positive, and shed a good light whenever someone is criticizing another. It makes you look good and also, it's the behavior that others will respect.

Don't blame others

The fastest way to obtain a bad reputation is to blame others for mistakes made. It takes a very strong person to take responsibility for their own errors. When people hear that you take responsibility, they are more forgiving than you think. Taking responsibility for your own mistakes is a respectable thing, and others will see you in a positive way. You will appear as a normal everyday person, and not an egomaniac.

Organizations can be large, but word will get back to the wrong parties and you will create resentment if you are blaming someone for your own mistakes. They will not be as willing to support your efforts in the future, and it may invoke retaliations when the stakes are high, when they would have otherwise defended or supported you.

It is you who are responsible for the work your department performs so you must take the burden of the truth. The most successful leaders are those who are willing to remind others that they are not infallible. Respect comes from others seeing you as an equal and not as a liar.

CHAPTER SUMMARY

In this chapter, we've covered how to develop and maintain support and cooperation within your team and across the organization, and the critical components needed to ensure collaboration can occur among all groups in an effective manner.

5

The New Employee

CHAPTER OBJECTIVES:

- Ensure you appreciate the responsibility you hold for properly orienting and introducing a new employee

- Understand the psychological aspects of human relations in the introduction of a new employee

- Encourage you to develop a strategy to introduce and orient a new employee to your department

- Help your group accept a new employee

Consider psychology

In any tightly-knit organization, employees with seniority or longevity with the company are unconsciously hostile toward the new employee. Whether this stems from fear of the new employee's ability to "surpass" them due to natural competition or a natural resentment to any new and unknown presence being "injected" into the group, this hostility may be in the subconscious of people in your group whether they express it or not.

The resentment and distrust of a new employee comes at the height of the stress that a new employee is encountering; this is especially difficult for a younger, more aggressive employee that has not learned the art of dealing with others cordially.

It's very important that, as you introduce a new employee to the group, they have a friendly and understanding manager who listens and is available for them. You should put yourself into their shoes: the first day on the job is very scary and, many times, the new employee knows nothing about what lies ahead or the dynamics of the competition in your group. It is your job to greet new employees warmly, put them at ease, and make sure you are attentive to the need for this person to start the job in the right frame of mind.

Pre-introduction process

If you are creating a new position and the duties of this new person will take some of the duties away from an existing employee, ensure that you speak with that person and ask if they want that to happen or if the new employee should take another responsibility instead. This will ensure you don't lose an already valuable worker due to resentment over the parceling-out of their job.

Before you bring a new candidate into the organization, you should take the time to strategically plan with your team what the new role will do. Don't be scared of feedback, as it will ensure you don't cause dissent in your group. If you truly don't feel comfortable getting feedback, another option is to just talk individually with your team members and introduce the new job role. This will ensure that others have time to adjust to the change prior to the person actually being hired and will allow the change in their minds to occur more naturally.

Remember, people reject change unless they are socialized to the idea first. So if they feel they are involved, they will accept change with little to no backlash.

Team based interviews

During the interviewing process, make sure that you involve your team members, even if you end up making the decision yourself, their minds will at least be prepared for your decision and they will feel that you have respect for their opinions.

It's important that you perform this ritual of introduction so that you avoid causing your group to feel that you are ignoring their feelings or being unfair to their needs.

It is this act that allows the group to move forward psychologically and allows them to be more accepting of a new employee. Besides, if you get bad feedback from a majority of your group, it would not be wise or fair to the new employee to push him into a group that does not feel they are a good fit. It will make it much harder for your group to work harmoniously and will also lead to dissent towards you as their leader.

First impressions

The first impressions that any new employee gets during the first few weeks on the new job can make the future bright or bleak. A new employee's first days are what create his perception of the whole organization. The loyalty a new employee has to the company is built on this first introduction to the new job and the people he meets. A person takes this first impression of the organization into their mind and carries that throughout their employment with the company. This will mold how they react to the company, and whether their perception is good or bad. It can have lasting effects on the morale and work ethic of the employee as well as how hard they will be willing to work. Keep in mind that it is "hope" that drives humans to achieve greater heights and produce harder, so this hope must be fostered right away.

When a new employee starts, you should take time to communicate to your team members that you expect them to go out of their way to make the new employee feel welcome. By doing this, you set the expectation of the group and they will feel responsible to uphold morale.

Improper induction

The results that you will have to face if you don't follow this simple process will be severe. They can include:

- Dissent

- Low morale

- Disloyalty

- Accidents

- Low productivity

- Employee turnover

- Time-wasting by the group

- Extended time needed for the new employee to become productive

- Anger and resentment towards you and the new employee An important aspect to keep in mind while going through the introductions with the new employee is that he may be:

- Scared

- Overwhelmed

- Tired and confused

- Anxious to start working on a task

- Unable to retain information received during introductions

Show interest

During his first few weeks on the job you should show interest in the new employee's personal affairs, needs, and wishes on a personal level. An effective way of doing this is to discuss hobbies or activities outside of work; it will put them at ease to know that you are human too. Tell them about yourself and what things you like to do after work.

I've heard many people tell me that being a friend to an employee is the wrong thing to do. Well, there is some truth to that. Don't go overboard, but at least be friendly enough so that they will trust you. This goes a long way in creating a productive environment for your new employee. Everyone in your group should be friendly enough with each other so that mutual trust can be established. This is what makes a group prosper and work harder for you, so don't forget it.

Proper point of view

Establish a proper point of view for the new employee. Make sure you compliment his resume and accomplishments. Even during the first few assignments you should make a point of saying "thanks" for their work. During a staff meeting, you might even bestow some praise over their latest accomplishments; you don't have to give out awards, just a little recognition. This will let the person know you have confidence in them and more than likely will lead to them working harder and with even better quality. This is the time to start building positive attitudes and loyalty.

New employee roles and responsibilities

You should instruct the employee on the work expected of them. Don't wait to start giving them things to do. You should be ready with tasks to start them on right away; this makes it easier for a person to adjust to their new surroundings and takes their mind off the awkwardness of being new. Even if the tasks you give are not very complex or intensive, it's important for you to indicate that these tasks are important. When you do this, you'll make them feel important inside.

Environmental introduction

You should properly show the person around to the different duty stations as soon as they are onboard. I know this sounds silly, but there shouldn't be any mystery regarding where to find the bathroom, common supplies, or the tools needed for the job. This ensures they can be self-reliant and productive from the first day.

Uncertainty on the job is bad for anyone, and worse for a new employee. The added stress created by this uncertainty can result in antipathy toward the job and even boredom! Make sure they know where to find the tools they needs to start being productive.

Explanation of duties

At the beginning stages, it's always advisable to tell the employee as much as you can about the work they will be performing. You must make them aware that everything they will fit well into the goals of the entire department. Sit down with them and explain what the department is doing as a whole and the strategy you have for accomplishing these goals.

This gives the employee a broad picture of the process and inspires them to take responsibility for, and a personal interest in, their contribution to the team's goals.

The hand off

Normally, in most departments you'll have an old timer in the group that you rely on for instruction and mentoring. Tell the senior employee that you'll be handing off some mentoring tasks to bring the new employee up to speed. This will make your veteran employee feel both trusted and important, and it will give the new employee another person besides you who can help resolve the issues that arise from day to day. You will be lowering your own workload for medial questions and answers, and this allows you to focus on your own duties.

Follow up

Towards the end of the day, follow up on the progress of the mentoring. Ask the new employee how things are going. This makes the new employee feel that you've not left them behind and that you value the experience that they are having; it also allows you to keep in touch with any issues that you need to address that the new employee is facing. Any issues during the first few weeks of their employment can affect their long term view of both you and the company. This is also a good opportunity to share a positive assessment of their work, and to share any new information that the employee may need. So take the time to follow up; it will be time well spent!

First assignment

The very first assignments given to an employee should be selected carefully. Start out with simple tasks, but customize them to the skills the new employee brings to the group. Don't try to teach everything on the first day because, more than likely, they won't remember everything you're trying to impart. It takes a person time to adjust and understand what their role is.

The tasks you assign should be relevant work and not remedial unless, of course, the employee needs to go through some safety training or other prerequisite instruction before the task is started. The tasks should be sequenced in such a way that they make sense. This helps the employee do the task correctly without causing problems or safety issues. Make sure the work is done the right way the first time through, if the work is physical make sure it's done safely.

Employee orientation & handouts

Normally, in larger companies, there is an established orientation class. If your company has one, make this the first thing an employee completes before you start giving out tasks. New employees should have all the necessary handouts and paperwork so that they can obtain the necessary information for insurance coverage, retirement benefits, stock options, or anything else being offered by the company.

The orientation should cover policies, regulations, and prohibitions in the workplace. Encourage questions about the information and make sure the employee receives either a prompt (and correct) response or the name of the person or department who has the answer. The orientation should also go over the products/services of the company as well as its history. An understanding of the organizational structure within the company can be very important for a new employee as well.

If your company doesn't have an official orientation procedure, take the time to go over these things with the new employee. It will increase his efficiency by allowing them to navigate and communicate to the rest of the organization.

Assess employee integration

You should review the following list to determine if you've properly introduced the new employee. Does the new employee …

• Feel like a part of your group?

• Realize his importance to the department?

- Have confidence in you, the company, and the work?

- Know the company policies, prohibitions, and reasons for them?

- Feel open to coming to you or your group mentors for information?

- Have a good attitude towards the company and his work?

- Have a desire to learn the job and work hard?

- Produce quality work efficiently?

- Get along with others on your team?

- Show loyalty to the department and your organization?

CHAPTER SUMMARY

In this chapter, we've reviewed how to appropriately bring a new employee into the group and how to ensure that the employee gets to work quickly and efficiently by meeting the team and being integrated into the organization.

6

Training Principles

CHAPTER OBJECTIVES:

- Learn the importance of training
- Develop a manager's mentoring and teaching abilities

A "Great Manager" is a good teacher

Your success as a manager will be determined by others based upon your ability to get your employees to accomplish their tasks or goals efficiently and with quality. Therefore, it is important that you train your employees well. It has been my experience that a great manager is one who always takes the time to give good instruction. People in general will naturally follow someone who helps guide them, and shows them respect by teaching them.

You should take a large portion of your time and dedicate that to teaching, mentoring, and instructing your employees on how to perform their duties better. Don't be scolding or come off rude; be respectful, and if you see someone doing something wrong, point it out by saying "You know, I think I know a better way to do that task, I would suggest trying …" This is a non-threatening and enjoyable way for others to learn.

Teaching is an art

Many people believe they are a good teacher simply because they know every part of a certain topic, or they know how to do something with ease. A more important thing to remember is that keeping someone open to suggestions and your instruction is not achieved by simply telling people how to do something, but by instructing them in such a way as to keep them open and interested in the topic on which you are instructing. Keep this in mind the next time you go to teach others.

A single misspoken word can turn a person's brain off or send his thoughts on a tangent or create resentment. Keep your words relevant to the subject at hand and keep your language and demeanor from being personal in nature. During any sort of instruction, it is always recommended to be light-hearted and find the humor in the repetitive or mundane aspects of a given task. This helps keep the mind of your trainee focused and alert.

During any sort of training session, you should always prepare some sort of handout material that summarizes your training so that it can be used to refresh your employee's memory when the need arises. If you know how to use PowerPoint, it's a great tool for either print or video display presentations during training. When using PowerPoint, or other training materials, make thorough use of examples. Examples will go far to show a particular thought or convey a message to your audience.

Ways to instruct

Managers, just like any employee in a company, are responsible for understanding the job at hand and determining the requirements to get tasks and goals completed. This differs from an individual contributor role.

A manager is responsible for the employees within his own department to ensure that the employees are properly trained. A manager must provide instruction so that the employees are following the proper methodology, process, or regulations that apply to a particular job.

Some examples of how a great manager instructs are:

1. **Ad-Hoc Instruction**—an employee asks for the information or the manager observes the employee doing something wrong and provides constructive feedback to the employee.

2. **Step-by-Step Tasking**— an employee may sometimes be instructed on what, when, and where they are supposed to complete a certain task. This depends on the industry you are in and the seniority of the employee, of course.

3. **Explaining Regulations**—Sometimes instruction may come from regulations and procedures that must be followed. For example: An airline pilot must check his ailerons and flight systems in a certain order when preparing for flight.

4. **Special Meetings**—From time to time, a special meeting is held to ensure that everyone is on the same page, per se. often these meetings cover new services, safety protocols, procedures, regulations, or new products being launched by the organization.

5. **Organized Instruction**— a manager may choose to create an organized class in-house for the employees that need to get some special training.

Common training mistakes

- Teaching to much all at one time.

- Teaching too fast.

- Not instructing from the employee's perspective.

- Not properly judging the person's response to the subject matter or questions that arise.

- Not being patient.

- Not adapting the training to the individual's learning capabilities.

- Not keeping the employee(s) interested.

- Not having fun and being tactful.

- Trying to teach an adult like a child.

- Not finding out what jobs the person has had before.

- Making assumptions that the person doesn't know the work.

- Not following up on instruction goals.

- Teaching without showing step-by-step progression to more complex tasks.

- Lack of preparation.

Who is responsible for developing the training?

Many corporations have centralized training departments that coordinate both internal and external training. They are normally responsible for creating classes for the various departments in the organization or coordinating the delivery of training to your employees. If your company does not have a training department, the responsibility will fall to you.

Keep in mind that if your company does have a training department, you are still responsible for your own employees' training. It may be best to do on-the-job training from within your own department. The training can be performed either by you or delegated to a senior staff member. Be sure that you are confident that your line manager or team lead can properly train your employees. Often, a team lead can be sent to an external training, bring back materials from it and create an informal or impromptu class to disseminate the information to the others on your team.

Use the points below to determine if you need training in your department. Any more than five of these behaviors should indicate you need to take action.

- Poor quality of work

- Low productivity

- Low morale

- Employees not loyal

- Excessive turnover

- Absenteeism

- Grievances or complaints

- Bickering over the lines of authority and jurisdiction

- Poor safety

- Poor housekeeping

- Lack of succession planning

- Manager doing operational work rather than delegating

CHAPTER SUMMARY

If you are a manager then you are a very pivotal figure in the training of your employees. You should consider yourself a teacher, because you are one. Good instruction can go a very long way to both improving your team and building morale. I would say that the most valuable trait in a leader is his ability to teach others properly. It is this ability that gives a manager the most efficient—and most loyal—staff.

7

Handling Grievances and Complaints

CHAPTER OBJECTIVES:

- To define your responsibility for the handling of complaints and grievances

- To shed light on the human side of grievances

- To make a productive employee from an unhappy employee

Importance of Handling Grievances

It is extremely important that every manager know how to properly handle grievances and complaints. It would be impossible to estimate the tremendous loss in production and morale resulting from countless minor complaints and grievances improperly handled by management. During the course of any employee's experience at a company, there are bound to be grievances. If a manager does not adequately address the problem it can turn into a highly disruptive force in the department.

When an employee brings a grievance to a manager or supervisor it should not reflect badly on them and these grievances should be taken seriously and acted upon in a professional manner. It takes much courage for an employee to approach management with a grievance, so these things should not be taken lightly. The initiation of a grievance should also not reflect badly on the employee's management unless multiple grievances have been received regarding a supervisor's or a manager's actions or activities.

Defining a grievance

A grievance could be anything about the job which irritates, upsets, or annoys an employee, or a situation where the employee believes that his working conditions are unsatisfactory. There will be many times when an employee will not tell you when he has a grievance. Rather than hearing it directly from the source, you may hear about a grievance through a coworker. Sometimes a grievance may exist only inside a person's mind; never expressed publicly or even privately.

Even though handling grievances is a tough task, it is important that a manager understands that sometimes it is necessary for employees to have the opportunity to speak openly about their frustrations. It is necessary for a manager to routinely schedule meetings or events that allow for the openness of communication.

The psychology of grievances

Many employees will not tell you that they have a grievance. The employees that will come to you are typically not afraid, those that won't come to you are afraid in some way. Some are afraid you'll be angered, upset, or seek retribution if they complain. Many people don't want to be labeled as troublemakers and so they just keep to themselves.

It is important to extract this type of information by either setting up a brain-storming session in which the group can list the problems that exist so improvements can be made. Another method in extracting this information is to set up one-on-one conversations with each of your employees. When you meet with each employee you must be direct, respectful, and nonjudgmental.

You must ask them to let you know what issues or challenges they are having, tell them they can feel comfortable that you trust them and that you will maintain privacy. Ignoring bad conditions in the department will make your employees feel unimportant and alienated. You must be on your toes and take action before your employees complain about you or your department to your management.

Even if you are a very good manager and are on top of everything there are still bound to be some situations that occur. It could be said that if you hear nothing things may be really bad. The morale of your entire department can hinge on whether or not its members feel free to approach you. If this is not the case, you must address this by looking inward on your personality or obtaining external opinions from a 360 degree review by your peers to understand better how to adapt so that others feel more at ease when approaching you.

A common mistake that managers make is they are not lighthearted enough around their subordinates to ensure that their subordinates feel as though management is on their side, ready to help them and address the issues they are having in an effective way. Employees will not come to you if they feel you will do nothing about their complaint.

If no channels exist for an employee to vent these frustrations with management, the problem will become magnified and soon an employee will likely quit or become negligent in his duties due to low morale.

Sometimes you'll find the quietest person becomes angry and blows up because of this lack of an effective communications channel. The communications channel serves as an outlet for the employee and an input to management to make changes where necessary so it is extremely important.

The great manager provides every opportunity to let employees vent their frustrations. They encourage them to come to them and seek their guidance or understanding. A great manager listens well and lets the person speak their mind. Psychologists commonly point out that the amount of frustration and anger can be significantly reduced if the person is given the opportunity to speak about their grievance. Much of the time a person can even solve their own problem when talking through the issue and venting their frustration with management.

The key to handling a grievance is to listen very carefully and not interrupt or try to respond until the person has completely explained their grievance. Give your employees every opportunity to speak and you will have a very stable group.

The Grievance Procedure

Accept responsibility

Most of the trouble from a grievance stems from the lack of a manager taking responsibility to listen to, and empathize with, the person grieving. Certainly none of us like to hear complaints about anything, because it makes us happy when others are happy and makes us uncomfortable when others are not. It is very common for managers to push problems to others or to blame others when, in fact, they should take responsibility. It is your responsibility to hear what the grieving employee has to say.

Listen

Put your employee at ease and make him feel welcome to come to you. Show that you are willing to be receptive and that you really care about how they feel. Show that they are important by paying attention to them directly.

Avoid

- Playing with your computer, cell phone, or other electronics

- Answering the phone

- Looking around the room

- Reading papers in front of you (unless provided by the employee for the grievance)

- Showing emotion

- Being defensive

- Arguing

Ask questions

Get the entire story by asking questions of your employee. You will both gain a better understanding of the problem and the employee will believe you are truly interested in it by asking simple questions. You may need to ask questions of others to determine the facts. Make sure you have all the facts before you make a decision. Sometimes people come with grievances that are not entirely accurate, so the process you use to ask questions and investigate will ensure you make fewer mistakes. If the griever knows you are going to verify all the facts there is less of an inclination for them to lie, fabricate, or embellish the story.

Inform management

Depending on the issue being raised, you may want to notify your own management that there is a grievance. You should let them know that you will handle the issue. Keep them informed of the progress of the grievance if necessary. This will ensure that if they hear about the issue from others, they will not overreact or be caught off guard.

Your management may want to become directly involved if the grievance or its solution is more universal to the company rather than localized within your particular department. Your management could even possibly solve the problem in conjunction with you or shed some light on the situation that may come from a past experience that they've had in dealing with that specific issue.

Make decisions

Once the first four phases of the grievance process are complete we can turn to one of the most important steps: making decisions. Making decisions will often affect the employee directly. At this point you should have carefully considered all the facts and come to a reasonable conclusion regarding both the reason for the grievance and the best solution to it. It is often difficult to make a decision but it must be made swiftly so that the employee feels that he is not being ignored and that the problem has had the proper attention given to it.

Keep in mind that sometimes a solution may impact one person in a positive way but others in negative ways so you must think thoroughly through the effect your decision will have on others in the group. Take time to think about each angle and how each person would perceive the solution based on your total knowledge of the person, their job role, and their typical interactions with others.

When presenting your decision, calmly explain to the employee the reasons for your decision. Often times going through all of the facts that led you to that decision with the employee will help them understand, and even possibly change, your decision before you communicate it to the rest of your team. Having the facts will allow you to defend your decision if necessary. It is best to try not to argue with your employee but simply state your decision. This is often done in a one-on-one meeting prior to disclosure to the rest of your team assuming that your decision affects them.

Provide open ended decisions

Keep your decisions open ended. What I mean by open ended is that the employee and the group have been given the "okay" to come to management and dispute or ask for changes to your decision. The effect this has is the group feels that the solution is created collaboratively and with at least some consideration for each of their respective feelings and roles on your team.

By giving your crew the thought that they can provide input, they will feel respected and this will result in building morale for the team and breaking down the walls between them and management. Demonstrating your own open-mindedness, you will attain higher levels of appreciation and respect from your team.

Follow Up

Make sure that at a later date you follow-up with the employee. This helps ensure that things are on the right track and you can avoid any additional issues in the future. Sometimes you'll find that there are additional pieces of information that are quite insightful. I've witnessed an employee even help solve their own issues while I was trying to address it from another angle. This process can be quite pleasing if you handle yourself carefully.

Chapter Summary

In this chapter, we've covered how to properly handle grievances, group dynamics to consider when handling them, and how to verify that the grievance has been effectively addressed.

8

Selecting the Right Employee

CHAPTER OBJECTIVES:

- Learn how to properly interview applicants

- Establish the importance of mapping an employee to the right task

- Provide guidance on the elements you must take into consideration when assigning an employee to a task

Getting the job done

As a manager, you are now held responsible for ensuring the job gets done. This includes the burden of getting the right individuals to accomplish the tasks at hand. It will quickly become obvious that you need to think carefully when considering who you should hire or assign to a job.

The interview is the most important process to go through in selecting the right person, so you should take the time to understand a candidate's strengths and weaknesses as this person's performance will directly reflect on your competence as a manager. Next, we'll focus on preparation steps necessary to do the interview process correctly.

Preparation

- Be in the proper mindset to conduct an interview.

- Set aside all other pressing issues and focus all your attention towards the goal of selecting the proper person.

- Have a set of not more than 10 questions or points you wish to convey in the interview process.

- You'll need to ensure you stay within a time window. I recommend one-hour interviews. Some managers prefer a half-hour, but you'll want to know as much as possible about this person before making a decision.

- Read through the resume. Pick several points of interest and review the candidate's history; you'll be able to pull questions and expand on each point by using their resume as a guide.

- Pick questions you want answered in advance of the interview. Unless the job requires immediate technical know-how, try to stick to topics broader in nature as most applicants can be trained after being hired.

During the Interview

The introduction

1. Introduce yourself and describe your job role; most applicants will be nervous to some degree and, if they know who you are and some of your background, this will put them at ease and helps them open up to you.

2. Act interested even if you are not; demonstrating interest in the words of another person is a form of respect. Extending this courtesy, whether deserved or not, reflects well on you.

3. While speaking with them, try to find common ground. This helps put aside any fears and makes you easy to interact with. I find that talking about how hard it is to interview is a good ice-breaker; I've even successfully repeated a joke or two to lighten the atmosphere.

4. Ask questions in a caring way. Show that you are also a person; if you end up hiring this person it will make for an easier transition when integrating them into your team and organization.

Build confidence

- Put yourself in their shoes, how would you perceive the interaction?

- Listen with interest

- Don't cross-examine like a court, and don't show suspicion; its rude.

Inform them of the job duties

- Keep in mind that the interview works both ways; you and the company are being sized up by the person across the table!

- Share information such as the pay rate, responsibilities of the position in question, and benefits available to employees.

- If there is a possibility of advancement, disclose this as well.

Get all the facts

- Before you decide whether or not to hire this candidate, get all the facts ironed out ahead of time.

- Evaluate their past experiences.

- Find out their goals and ambitions.

- Determine what their strengths and weaknesses are.

- Analyze his personality; this is an important one since this can be a key factor in determining on-the-job performance. Watch out for slackers!

Observe them carefully

- Try to be as impartial as possible, try to conduct yourself as if you didn't have any hang-ups or opinions formed.

- Familiarize yourself with Federal and State Law regarding the hiring process; there are questions you absolutely _cannot_ ask during an interview and they aren't all confined to politics or religion.

- Try to separate yourself from what you see and hear; this will allow you to evaluate without prejudice.

- Listen carefully and contentedly.

- Keep a finger on the pulse of the interview; make sure it does not get too intense. Nervousness can be determined by body language.

- If the candidate appears exceedingly nervous, change the topic briefly and talk about yourself, shift the focus away from them for a moment.

- Be sympathetic to his feelings and you'll be on your way to achieving great success.

How to ask questions

- Keep your questions as clear as possible.

- Unless you're the District Attorney, do not play word games or use questions as an ambushing tactic; it's an interview, not an interrogation.

- Do not word your questions in a way that elicits a particular response, most people will try to come up with the answer they think you want to hear rather than the truth.

- Ask questions one at a time so as not to overwhelm them.

- Start with easy or general questions and slowly build the interview's intensity; this will keep them from feeling off-guard and will provide you with more thoughtful answers.

- If they mention something of interest to you, follow their lead, this will more than likely shed important light on their experiences and promote openness of the discussion.

- Avoid trick questions, again getting back to fairness; you should be focused on finding the right employee, not searching for a way to reject the person in front of you.

- Be approachable and allow the candidate to ask questions.

Start a discussion

It's always important to give the interviewee a chance to just talk and share perspectives. This allows the person to open up and get to know you better. It also sheds light on areas that you may have missed during the questioning phase. I know it sounds corny, but you could even talk about the weather or recent news to open things up. I found this to be an effective way to move the discussion away from work and expose the candidate's personality and interests.

Close the interview

- If you can, inform them of your decision.

- If you are performing a group interview, let them know that they'd be a good candidate if selected and that someone will inform them whether or not they will get the job.

- Follow the rules of good social conduct; a handshake, a smile, and sincere thanks for the candidate taking the time to come in and be interviewed.

- Show empathy for the interviewee's perspective during the interview by thanking them for putting up with your questions; this sends them out with a better feeling even if you don't select them for the position.

- In all ways, give the impression that the candidate will receive a "fair shake" when you consider whom you will hire.

- No matter how unlikely it may seem, always bear in mind that you might end up working for the person you just interviewed.

Final assessment

Things to look for in the candidate you just finished interviewing:

- Motivation

- Loyalty

- Alertness

- Positive attitude

- Open-mindedness

- Observant

- Initiative

- Ability to learn

- Ability to grow

- Enthusiasm

- Common sense

- Ability to integrate with your existing team

- Honesty and trustworthiness

- Reliability and longevity

- Personal pride in accomplishments

- Interest in the job

- Reasons for wanting the job

Selecting the right person for the role

Next, we'll talk a bit about what considerations you should give when selecting the right employee for the role you need performed. This is a very important step because it will determine if you, as the manager, and the employee, as your subordinate, are both happy with the outcome. An unhappy employee will misrepresent the position and reflect badly on you. A properly selected employee will make your reputation soar and your employee grow.

This process is somewhat analogous to farming: A farmer wants the best seed sown into the best fields. The soil needs to be prepared, the seeds sown, and then, from time to time, it will need to be checked for growth, strength, and success.

There are very similar paradigms to management and farming. You need to care for people and really work for their growth and then you'll succeed in having a beautiful plant which will produce excellent fruit.

Utilize the employee's strengths

It's been said that a good leader makes more leaders. Leadership is the most important aspect of selecting an employee for a position. You must assess an employee's skills, and then select a role that you believe will utilize all of their experience. It should be a role that the employee can eventually lead.

Delegate the work to the right person!

Far too many managers I've known over the years end up doing most of the work themselves despite having very capable people in their department. It's important to know how to properly delegate work to the appropriate person. Doing all the work yourself is not the name of the game. As a manager, it's your job to manage the work across the people underneath you; not do it all yourself. Fit the task to the person and delegate. It's difficult sometimes to trust others, but this is an essential part of the job. Knowing who to delegate to should be based on strengths and weaknesses. It's your job to know where each employee fits into the picture.

Maximizing the employee's abilities

In general, you should always maximize the utilization of your employee's strengths within the job role. Employee motivation is derived from the satisfaction of going home at the end of the day feeling that meaningful work was accomplished. If you properly assign an employee, he will have real satisfaction with the company, your department, and themselves.

The Leader

If you have someone who shows real interest in leading, give them creative things to do within that area of responsibility. This is important because normally a person wants to be promoted when he feels they can contribute beyond their current role. It's up to you to cultivate that leadership and prepare that person for leading. There's nothing wrong with having leaders under you and delegating some of your own decision-making to them as team leads.

The Planner

If you have someone who likes to plan things out and is very strategic, you should utilize that interest and delegate the scheduling and planning work for the team.

Use that person's strengths as a strategic planner and have them help develop the departmental plans and goals.

The Perfectionist

Utilize this kind of employee for reviewing work. This will help increase the efficiency and quality of the work that is being performed by the department.

The Socialite

Socialites can be best delegated as liaisons between your team and other departments. "People skills" is often the punch line to job-related humor, but these skills do, in fact, come in handy for the person you choose to represent you and your team.

The Analyst

The Analyst is a meticulous problem-solver who enjoys the challenge of finding a solution when it isn't already patently obvious. Some teams don't have this function, so it's good to be creative with these types of people. An analyst likes to look at many aspects of a problem and apply reason and logic to discover possible solutions. I've often benefitted from analysts; receiving insightful information and thereby implementing better solutions than what I would have devised on my own. They enjoy the challenge, and I enjoy the information; it's a truly win-win situation.

Employees normally do best in situations that utilize their education and experience to the fullest extent. Your success will be based on the ability to assess these employees and uncover any desires they may have. I've found that one-on-one discussions are the best forum for exploring an employee's desires. You'll want to keep this information file on your employee. I've found it's also good to even create a spreadsheet to track the abilities of your team. This will also help your replacement if you decide to move to another job or to another company during the turnover process.

Assess and address weaknesses

As with all of us, we sometimes have weaknesses, at one time in my life I taught week-long certification courses. After the first day of teaching, I would assess my class. If I had class members that had considerable difficulty in the course or the labs, I'd take steps to address this issue.

One solution was to approach a more successful student and ask if they would do a little on-the-fly mentoring. The better student got a feeling of importance and usefulness, and the struggling student got much needed help. Applying the same solution to members of your team will give the same win-win results.

On other occasions, when you don't have the luxury of sparing a top-per-former, your best option would be to send the underperforming employee to some sort of training. Employees are often intimately aware of their shortcomings and they will smell the reek of insincerity if you pretend the training is "policy" or "commonplace". Deliver the news from the perspective that the company sees them as being worth the investment of added training.

Job safety

Job safety is hardly more than a poster in some companies and literally life-or-death in others. If your company leans more toward the latter, you should be on the lookout for signs of incompetence, laziness, and carelessness at all times, including the interview.

It's true that many companies rate employee on how their safety history has been, and sometimes even bonuses or pay are based on it. Controlling danger means reducing risk, and this requires you to put the right people in the right positions for the safety of everyone on the team.

Assess their temperament

A quick fuse or bad attitude can make for a disaster between and within groups.

Endeavor to place a person in situations that will improve their temperament rather than make it go out of control. You'll need to address this by identifying the causes of the bad temperament. Most often it is caused by a person's principles and values.

CHAPTER SUMMARY

In this chapter, we've covered the different types and personalities of employees and how to properly select the right one for a particular task. This will ensure you have each employee applied in the most efficient manner and should greatly enhance your ability to deliver for your organization.

Conclusion

With these fast changing times, one thing that does not change is human relationships. We all want to feel important, accomplished, successful, and competent in one area or another in our lives. It's our role as managers to guide our employees. Allowing them to constantly grow during their employment and foster a positive atmosphere for their work. Do your best for people and they will do their best for you. Show you care about others and they will care about you. In the end you'll be remembered as a good, easy going, and compassionate individual who has contributed to the success of others with humility.

Notes

Notes

Notes

Notes

Notes

Notes

www.ingramcontent.com/pod-product-compliance
Lightning Source LLC
Chambersburg PA
CBHW030859180526
45163CB00004B/1636